Pop music jingles, statistics, the frames of text and camera selecting the world's headlines for our perusal, a stroll along the Champs Elysées jammed against the slum of Kibera—*A Bad Year for Journalists* feeds the jagged, seductive language of media into the emotional cusinart lived by the media's flawed though courageous practitioners. To say
what it was
not what it was like.

Also by Lisa Pasold:

Weave

A Bad Year for Journalists

Lisa Pasold

Frontenac House
Calgary, Alberta

Book and cover design: Epix Design
Cover photo: Neil Petrunia
Author photo: David Scollard

Library and Archives Canada Cataloguing in Publication

Pasold, Lisa
A bad year for journalists / Lisa Pasold.

Poems.
ISBN 1-897181-01-9

I. Title.

PS8631.A825B343 2006   C811'.6   C2005-907655-0

We acknowledge the support of the Canada Council for the Arts which last year invested $20.3 million in writing and publishing throughout Canada. We also acknowledge the support of The Alberta Foundation for the Arts.

 Canada Council   Conseil des Arts
for the Arts   du Canada
 Alberta
Foundation
for the Arts

Printed and bound in Canada
Published by Frontenac House Ltd.
1138 Frontenac Avenue S.W. Calgary, Alberta, T2T 1B6, Canada
Tel: 403-245-2491   Fax: 403-245-2380
editor@frontenachouse.com   www.frontenachouse.com

1 2 3 4 5 6 7 8 9 11 10 09 08 07 06

For Bremner

Acknowledgements

For encouragement & thoughtful suggestions, a thousand thanks to Bremner Duthie, Lauren B. Davis, Jennifer K. Dick, Rhonda Douglas, Jennifer Huxta, Greg Kruse, Michelle Noteboom, Joe Ross, Todd Swift, Russell Wangersky, Cecilia Woloch, and everyone at the Banff Centre Writing Studio. Thanks also to Sparkle Hayter for permission to quote from her upcoming novel *Last Girl Standing*, and to John Darnielle for permission to quote from The Mountain Goats' song "Raja Vocative". And thanks to the Canada Council for an extremely helpful grant which allowed me to finish this manuscript.

A traveller's gratitude goes to Joanna Wedge & Mike Crawley in Nairobi, Nadine Sivak & Colin Taylor in Kensington Market, Colleen Kappel in Thunder Bay, the barbeque-ers extraordinaire in Calgary, and my parents Anne & Peter Pasold in Gaspé.

Excerpts from this collection have appeared in *New American Writing* (issue 23, 2005), nthposition.com (January 2005) and *Talking Down the Mountain* (2006). *Merci à tous.*

Contents

"Between 9-11, Al Qaeda, Iraq, and an apocalyptic White House, the events of my life in Paris hardly seemed worth recording. While my friends were walking through minefields and DMZs to report the news, work for peace or bring succor to the suffering, I was in Paris, doing work that didn't matter one whit in the grand scheme of things in a place that seemed about as real as Brigadoon."

- Sparkle Hayter, *Last Girl Standing*

true or false, what did reach her? pretending to dream, she
murmurs *sale métier*. her eyes open.

the word was *sailor*. or maybe *salvation*. worn-out streets,
walking meditation.

without defenses. with shoes, with gloves.
they don't pay enough to make her honest. she'd like to feel bad
about that.

(the collaborative angels have cabin fever, they're
fed up with floating, untouched, they want
more than spiritual dialogue. they're tired of making
excuses for the human race.)

it was on BBC, it must be true. she's perusing
websites, compiling stats, a neurotic hobby of distress:

    63 journalists killed worldwide in 2005 (not only in Iraq)

numbers with the artistry of the silversmith's apprentice.

    1,146 reporters threatened (keep moving. don't look back)

alternately,
there are the hostages. there's a trick to it, no denying. sad dumb luck.
keep working. keep moving.
and?

the pitch. the hook. the story. she's on the phone long distance.

speaking for the angel

what the hell was she thinking? dented metal suitcase requiem-like.
she looks, as from across the street:

                              professes

not to care. shiftless.

she's Goldie Hawn, in a Wong Kar-wai movie.
as good a place to start as any. she's wearing gold earrings.

                    accumulation.

the faces of those torn apart; she sets herself on automatic,
holds ice against the edge of something. a green green filter
in the flesh of memory.

grinding noise, something like a
soundtrack:

            airplane tickets in hand. passport. visa. presscard.

a different pair of shoes.

press

caterpillar mascara... these good-byes are so
tremendously flawed, she'd rather
not.

carry-on with wheels, light. even though
wheels aren't that useful
on dirt, the scunge of
plastic bags, waste.

what she's really carrying, there's no baggage check.

untaken photographs under her eyelids. each scene makes her
wince. *50 ways to leave your lover*, wormingly. inner ear
to the heart. the noise of the airplane doesn't
help. nor her Mormon
seat neighbour, who asks if she's interested in the Word.

depends on whose, she says, plugging in her earphones.

inflight movie, Angelina Jolie doing credit to her sports bra.
actually she's not
an idiot. just looks like she should be.

and okay, so she likes that look. is it her fault
politically correct never turned her on? apparently.
lipstick, and a Dayton to the groin. something predictable like that.

she falls asleep to the turbulence, nausea
familiar.

something's blurring
at the edges. the scene drifting both ways at once, she's not
a fast-moving train. *isn't that just
typical of you*, damn voice in her head. how many lovers
does it take to give her distance? oh it's snowing, it's simply
snowing. no. she pushes herself awake, the airplane
circling fog, pulling into what isn't there. white lack
of landscape.

taxi's driven by a Turkana, spots him towering.
tourist scrim and *matatus*. ah, Nairobi
(detours through high class Karen) a postcard tacked to a tentpole,
if she's asked. yeah, it's a picture.

she gets
to Emmanuel's borrowed house in time for breakfast.

he has on his English footballer looks though he remains
French. they always speak her language
except in front of other people.

he begins a long description of his dreams. she knows to be
noncommittal.

they discuss routes, conclude with
two thirteen-year-olds festooned in Russian-made
hardware. *do you have any idea how old those guns are?* as they get
in the back.

> they can each fit everything of value
> into a single suitcase, reduce
> to symbols of sentiment—

> Emmanuel carries his heart in his palm, like eyes. she
> keeps high-speed film in coat pockets.

they're friends even though
he's the palace-of-love kind of guy, and she's more *hello i'm leaving,*
your keys are on the counter.

> is that so
> surprising?

frangipani. impala. favoured, but not hers. not favourite to her.

the plane packed with khat leaves: lean against big green bales.

sounds belonging to other people
that she can't adopt.

      words like Kalifi. Lamu. or, she
      who is my beloved. or, that one with whom sugar
      has no need to melt.

she takes
photographs through the plane's open door, lock flung back for take-off
amidst gun-toting children. as if they
risk poachers, are a specific protected species. she tests
this out in French: not funny.

"prepared as a chewable paste or tea, the controlled-substance has side
effects including insomnia, anxiety, and suppression of appetite"

should pave this here road, says the taller kid as the plane bumps. skids.

      dust and vertigo.

getting in's worse than usual, that

baseball bat across the hood, after stopping. noticing

dark shapes under scrub. shadows, no trees, only
underbrush. crumbled pavement masquerading
as road, strip of rubber imbedded with nails, broken bottles. *what a pretty*

police barrier.

came this way this mornin', coupl'a hours ago. the driver mimes
self-assurance or desperation. at the boy's gesture, dash
against the gas pedal, hell yes.

don't look back or care about the dent in the jeep. *fuck it,* puts her knees
against the glove compartment, slouching. *i'm keeping my sunglasses on.*

hands unclenching inside her pockets.

camera under the seat.

what was once
(three stars? four?)
the Grand Hotel, very concrete. they drink Ethiopian coffee.
tiny cup. going over the rules:

    arms not exposed. never out alone. never at night.
    whatever she thought, they were sharing a room.

clarify: room,

    not bed.

(the moon rang against the metal of sky above an ocean still shallow, boats
 tide-beached.)

that "recrafted by force" look: the government spokesman, conniving.

assures them of what?

        that the Gu rains will come?

        that "food insecurity"
        cut off those refugees' hands?

they are driven to
a relief centre, aid distribution.
she turns the consonants around on her tongue. knows they are
inedible.

Emmanuel up front talking with the gun boys. making
them laugh.

this is part, or it is only:

867,000 people,

she tries to make a picture of it. impossible to get hold of.

okay, eight hundred thousand. she thinks of Kibera slum, Nairobi,
sea of brittle shacks swerving across that hill.

no, only 600,000 there.

mentally adds another face, and another.

after 12 years, finally this number small enough to hold in her hand,
coming home—*how could I not?* says one woman.

Emmanuel makes notes, two languages littered with camp slang.

we're so rational. a man stands still for her camera; his name
means "striking snake"
is it important, that particular detail?

Emmanuel sleeps in the minivan, his head thrown back.

invent guidebook titles: *Let's Go Mogadishu. Fodor's City Guide to Buulobarde.*

once upon a time.

dust from the window. they cross NO WEAPONS BEYOND
THIS POINT into camp. everyone is leaving.
there should be roadsigns, one way.

you let me befriend you, she thinks. *what's that,*
a kind of generosity?

such places are at their best dismantled

abandoned fields bloom with plastic bags, blue,
white, green.

the CNN announcer (can't bring herself
to call him a journalist, too camera-ready in his *oh for god's sake*
flak jacket) chats her up in the hotel lobby.

Emmanuel, with luggage, as if on cue.

        she notices his
        optimism,

        steps
        around it.

everyone turns up, the perfect media moment, equipped
with appropriate recording devices. there are cocktails and nibblies
served on silver platters by
beautiful waiters in poorly-fitted white jackets.

she says his mission
is to keep her drunk, it's a pact for these events. too sober
and she'll end up clocking
the minister. *not to say it wouldn't be deserved, but a brawl's just
too much work in high heels.*

Emmanuel laughs. he thinks
she's joking. bristling camera, lens, tripod, whatnot. *insouciant*
dishonest speeches; she frames obedient handshakes, ministerial poses.

repatriation...
"$40 per person. Plus blanket, cooking set, sleeping mat,
tarpaulin, hygiene supplies. Nine months of UN food rations"
...applause.

nine?

we are all to be new born whispers the Somalian writer.

you were too good
at keeping me drunk.

from the open edge of "God's Will" purple minivan.
she looks through his hands
as some failed future
leaks past. leaning out the window, no longer puking.

the driver skirts the ditch, brakes,
veers back.

her guts
stop spinning. *ça va mieux?* asks Emmanuel.

she recognizes regret. wanting
just the same.

sings *Your Southern Can*—under her breath.
Blind Willie McTell.

Emmanuel grouching at his laptop battery.
she shuffles lenses, stops; the hospital grounds:

   picnics, sheets airing, the very very thin.

something off-green.

   didn't learn anything useful
   in medical school
   he could only recognize
   tools—*shrapnel,* not the surface skin had been made into.

she nods,
positions the camera.

what changes.

   he gestures towards the press bus: *some of 'em seem to think*
   M.A.S.H. was reality TV. the doctor
   twists, *i'm supposed to have time*
   to explain?

unexpected influx.

headlines, ways to emphasize "global terrorism" (versus that other
less-marketable kind)

more people die in skirmishes. *it's technology,* the doctor tells her,
we get cell phones that don't work. Kalashnikovs that do.

guns come in from Ethiopia. they appear in the capital like
blossoms at specific times of year. he takes her to another wing.

close-up of wounds, some involving
children. *is what you wanted, isn't it?*

I don't need a lover, I
just need—he sees what he wants it
to be. she doesn't.

someone "warns the government to ease the nation's refugee crisis"

they always forget to explain...comment ils vont faire ça, he says.

the envoy's plane takes off as if levitating
straight off the dirt runway.

"the world's worst humanitarian disaster"

leaves them to bump back into town, to explain something
to somebody
somewhere else.

being good isn't always easy.

drinking coffee again. the driver's name is Fred.

Emmanuel trudges away, dialed-in reportage on schedule.
she adds more sugar.

you are like a cheetah—he is alone, says Fred,
all honesty. looking not
at her but at the solidly departing back of her colleague. *the cheetah
isn't large or wide—there are tears in his face.*

she wonders what tears at her.
a claw? a finger?

she puts the conversation back into professional gear.

the room dark with night, she surfaces. Emmanuel
is shouting
in his sleep, words not
taking shape as syllables.

    she gets up, crosses the concrete floor,

puts a hand
against his shoulder. a fist whips
to her neck's
pulse point. breath.

hook.

his hands around her throat. no
sound.

    he wakes up.

then this space, size of a small colour. left afterwards.

what proofs do we have to go on?

he writes to a word limit and collects his pay.

her photographs go out by wire service.

she doesn't sleep through the heat.

in the future morning, their usual move to a different country.

a wolverine's more like a rat than a bear

a sound he makes when down and wool. the way
those bombs went off, the special effectness.
slight changes inside

like a pig's eye. anticipating the wrong telephone call,
furtive. he promised to come back and look after me.
so look after me, I called.

exhausted and excused. face against pillow. head
against wall. hand against throat. over, past, at the corner.

all the clichés: put on Annie Lennox. figure out how to spell
heartbreak. something about intestines, I think. finer organs
strictly aren't involved. a bit of harpsichord stuck
in oesophagus, that's *it*, that's
what he meant. damn, if I'd only known. hands empty, fingers
held by water, smelling like gin. hell, wash the sheets.

the future before us

there's a trick to it, keep rollin' under fire. underneath what?
a romantic's way to say: some fucker's trying to...hang on, okay,
we're outta...

keep the dreams down, buddy. ya move fast enough, not even the dead
can keep up with ya. think *Pulp Fiction* was joking? freakin' movie
every time i'm in back of a jeep, some kid's holdin' a machine gun.

what with the suntan, the glare here.
a genocide doesn't suddenly stop like a football game.

drivin' down the street, the soldiers start screamin'. kinda a snap decision:
drive like hell, or stop because it's an official checkpoint?
might be they're gonna shoot us even if we do stop. and if
they're lookin' for something expensive to kidnap? that would be me.

i never know. livin' isn't honest.

what i like about blowin' things up? how clean it is, afterwards.

a heavy dose of fear and violence, yep, you'll convince these guys.
good luck, buster-jangle.

tried a desk job, christ i went mental, missed the field. this is
my retirement plan.

everything telescopes. sing a national anthem?
save that for another country.

know why they invented Krazy Glue? skin wounds.
doctors in the field, the Korean War. gluein' the boys together,
fly 'em to surgery. no joke, buddy.

no, i've got every name. every photograph. this here's
Innocent Aevouelie. this is Bogdan Simic. here, Medhanie Haile.
i want names. so's i remember. Florence Kabeya.
Fred Ouaknine. Youssef Kouame.
you try wagin' peace, see how far ya get.

is it for the beauty of the land that we do not look upon it?

the blur of lipstick. timezones
as window shades. five dollars of J&B whiskey with turbulence.

we had different itineraries;
I got to Calgary without my luggage, cursing absent friends.

unable to decide if 29
made him less forgivable than 23?

she said "Nah
grass makes me puke. let's get a beer."

*

the short word, faith. my country and back again,
enough land to swallow us whole.

I welcomed myself home in every town:
differing drinks, variant conversations, a series of cafés

cocaine in the airport & back out on the plane
very rockstar, as if I still worked for Billboard.

*

of course it felt like being in love. stands to reason, a fallen angel
is beautiful and terrible.

we were walking down a summer street. just below the steps, bright blue
shirt open. a hint of smoke.

in the distance, roofers stepped from gable to chimney,
pebbles of rain against the flawed tin. was it so long ago,

striving and strutting?

weren't we like that though, bring it on, as much as we can take and
that little bit more.

everything we never and ever wanted, just a hand's reach. the keeper
of the infernal city.

we had this idea we were holding the other person upright.
then we drove away. how to explain the top hat or the wrist support
wrapped snake-like.

*

it was all laid out in the Times Literary Supplement but we had
no subscription.

"you look like a movie star.
 Sorry."

balancing coffee. a street guy sang *Noo York Noo York,*
if we can make it there, across the Kensington sidewalk in sunshine.

a wet scraggy dog running along the bank of the Bow River and us,
discussing Sylvia Plath, on May Day, this year.

*

we drove past whole fields of purple and rose lupins.

please, I exhaled. the breath was suspended, visible particles,
all humility and coolness. a photograph of the Arctic Watershed.

a pinch of fingers,
Loretta Lynn on the Buick's rattling stereo.

a piano came apart at the seams; you wept with pleasure.

and if we took a coarser approach to
honesty? the sounds that went down
the street, things frightening and desirable.

*

just finished with marriage, she was entitled to bad art
in her newly-sparse house. and us in the guestroom?

to describe the pulp mill, she held her hands palms out:
an abattoir
burning beside a lemon grove.

she said "each floor is a different donut, mine's a krueller." the view
from her window suggested
someone drowning.

that hooded shape, arms upturned.

over the strawberries and burned almonds and the basement flat.
on the radio, a woman's earnest CBC voice: "I felt the air prod
my breasts."

we held Bellinis that tasted like ketchup.

marooned in knitted
ambitions, we said, "So who were you?"

*

we knew we were addicts, the tracks marked up & down,
but my god it was very rarely
boring.

what to keep from that?

you can only take so much whispered against my neck. I think
i'm remembering this wrong.

she waved good-bye. we put what we could
in the trunk. we travelled
light, our pasts
tattooed across our hearts—for whatever good
were our opened hearts, if we wore no scars.

*

and yes, I turned my ankle with those pretty shoes,

but after so much work well done,
we were doing a job badly, how that was worthwhile too.

i can't stand it but i'm all right

a satellite phone, a tent, and $2,500 in cash,
wishing him the best, with a *bise* on the cheek.

it's what they call outsourcing, she said.

malaria was mostly real but he couldn't help focusing
on the machetes. got himself some mosquito netting, learned
how to remove leeches. not a problem.

                something about being expendable?

company policy was poorly
thought-through: his colleague driven through Abidjan,
all tinted-glass SUV
security with handguns loosely
against the armrest of the door—

               "target" in expensive tail-lights.

*

his editor says, *Ivory Coast ain't for sissies*, but at the same time
she shrugs, *want me to
pick you up some cheese while i'm in Paris?*

nods. though for himself, he says *Côte d'Ivoire*, as if it might be
less lethal in another language.

*

his morning routine's through town on foot,

wearing a pretty fine suit
made for him down the street, a tailor's market stall. he never fails
to say hello, passing by.

he considers anyone's likelihood of being inconspicuous.
his cousin. himself. the subtleties
of a passport.

> when someone falls into step beside him, his accent
> remains impeccable. a red line unravels in his eyes.

he promises to
see what he can do.
thinking, *if we all know we're lying, why do we keep on?*

*

boiling frog syndrome, says his editor, months later. Camembert
long gone. she closes the office windows. *explain to me
why the fuck we're still here?*

he says, *you know they only start shooting
after lunch.*

he listens to himself.

well, yeah, a boiling frog.

there are worse things.

they need a new
strategic plan.

something with cross-border opportunities, she says, *something
the Times won't bump to page 15.*

*

the absence of noise after 8pm, eeriness
of curfew. as if hearing
is better—*at least you know.*

when he can't sleep, he forces himself
to go over in his mind
the subtle differences between Stilton and Roquefort.

the textural contrast, the differing mould patterns & varying
consistency against crackers. the fact that he prefers
Swedish rye with cheese,
the crumbs & crunchiness superior to Melba toast.

usually he falls asleep
before getting to that detail.

every morning he walks out. unimaginable impunity,
where he'd rather not dare tread.

what's possible

"Hidden agendas: How journalists influence the news"
she reads. *that's just fan-*tas-*tic, I knew they'd get*
to blaming us one of these days.

it's a simple job,
"radicalizing the pain of others." Or selling it.

because she's there to make money
off their situation. at least,
they think she is.

> *can you sell this?*

so they throw shit at the car. their own shit. towards her.
splatter the windshield.

(if she worked, say, for FOX, she could skip
this, make it up as she went along. *like whistling a tune.*)

where's her handy
pith helmet and guidebook? in the Strand once
she came across *Directions for Englishmen*
Going to India. 19th century binding opened in her hand
to page 41. Bodoni Book font, smudged advice:

> "Stand still and wave a white handkerchief. This should
> confuse the elephant."

there was no illustration.

but the handkerchief remains, the elephant pauses
to decipher meaning

—truce? surrender? you're
about to blow your nose?—the elephant's hesitation
an opportunity:

Run. Run away.

Keep driving, she says now from the passenger seat.
Just keep driving.

Venus and Psycho, or,
I'd rather do it slowly as the bar graffiti says

one gold earring.

picture it spun like a top on the surface: he isn't mathematics fell. fallen. befallen.

becalmed.

make it simple: they met at an industry party, he was her
colleague's date. they got

to
talking.

remember, we met

cell phone hovering

oh,
I remember, she said.

Virgin megastore promo afternoon, the 7-to-13 market's very big here.
look
you're allowed to be cynical. wishes she still smoked, to hell with it
outside on the Champs Elysées wallowing.

phone texts and workman ethics. goes back inside to rattle procedure, sits
with the techies. expletives for the boy band, *all they have to do*
is photogenic

going over the previous night like what, coins?
looking at photographs. *should've printed*
lighter, the club just green-black background, twisting bodies.
dancing? blown to?

he's over Sudan right now. South Sudan. will land at Loki.

tries to find a taste to the word.

all so far away. literally, symbolically, another, somebody else's.

she tries to focus: band's done, done-in,
megastore crowd seeps off, people like so much water.
press pack talk, small mercy,

band manager with a rare
sense of humour, *saignant.*

buys her gin & tonic at Sir Winston. *you okay?* shakes her head, *yeah, fine* it's a week later, no, two weeks. call from the airport, *affection or efficiency?* embarrassed by how fast she can get to his place

Frida Kahlo's eyes, paste-up in the toilet, she pauses.

hotel room keys pinned
to the wall. he collects what exactly?

assume the worst. panama hat
tipped low over one brown eye, singing like Dusty Springfield

the least articulate person she's ever met. *articulated*, the way
hinges or joints fold together?

a reminder propped against the tattooed mug, as if he's already—

      one day

she's going to find herself blowing down the street.

flat on the edge of the city. third floor. *bugger*
love, what an inflatable santa. punches into the cushions.

sometimes
I don't know the
language
you're speaking, he says, hand across her face, rubbing her out or is he
memorizing

making pop songs pay the rent

she ambitions: a window seat, a corner desk, a gayer assistant.

office mail brings seven album covers,
all of them wrong, two videos, prepubescent. tries to feel *enthusiasmic*

that night dancing to Beyoncé & worrying the Grammys
in lamé higher heels. three martinis into the future, not
going home with the pretty suit tho he'd've been—

what's the point of waiting? roofless at dawn.

the journalists went on strike.
the news stopped happening.

he's too tall anyway. her fingers against his teeth, square & even. steady.
holding a lens, say. things are closer than they appear.
further?

piles of *objects*. she gets
objective. trying to see why
this is
in any way okay,

that it is.

arms, legs. shift from his sleeping, the sun
scratches. smell of salt or chemical, film.

don't look at me with the Mary Poppins
eyes, i'm flying out Monday.

                            she feels
                            insaisissable

wonders
if that's a good thing

would prefer to be weighed down, she could press against all present tense.

Dhafer Youssef on the iPod
World's going Techno-Urban, she says, *I like it.* caring about this,
yes, actually caring. because it's good. doesn't that matter?

passionate
about fluff?

cue the music.

she finds herself buying *Libération*. folds it small.

human triggers, headquarters pierced with paper. bulldozers.

photographs—*those thousand words*, digitized. what's left

unseen means unsaid?

unviewed, in daylight, unreported.

a dream of being hit in the head. a bad dream.

chocolate and T-shirt favours, *Hot Chocolate*
Christmas party at the Jaguar
showroom: *don't ask.*

flaming martinis, gogo girls on the hoods.

she gets blotto too quickly talking to celebrity VJs, one
with a fish-shaped birthmark
over his right shoulder blade,

okay so she found this out a little later.

maybe it was just a tattoo

in the midst, morning hangover mist, the cell phone

call from Djibouti, *I was wondering*
how you were doing

she takes
two aspirin, traces the route in the celebrity's bathroom.

crying from fatigue, *that's all*

invents excuses, leaves the VJ,
7 a.m. metro, home

wherever that is.

this conversation that does not occur is all one-sided. it sounds like this.
it takes place in her conditional.

look you can't just turn up

then disappear

and not call

then call

like that.

.

it does not take place, repeatedly.

through the month of April she reworks, forgets, most consciously.
with that much effort? *of course*

only a fool doubts.

something slipping, her body suspended. wanting to
rape whoever
turns up next.

bite into
skin,

her own.

long sleeves.

depression's
too many spam-advertised pharmaceuticals.

melancholic, better, heartbroken, yeah, very
goth, all Melissa Auf der Maur or possibly early Hole.
black nailpolish velour with torn stockings. she tries
Christian Dior
instead. orders the next gin & tonic,
lightens her hair, laments to few friends. they
do not ask. do not
notice? she

considers changing her phone number.

why bother, it's not ringing. until of course
it does. she doesn't answer.

      her assistant
dancing on his swivel chair. Pascal Obispo in pink feathers, *yeah*
    baby, this is really gonna work

    setting up the tour, faxing dates, got the song on repeat.

          when he fucking walks into
          her office.

every frivolity to judge her for—speakers the size of
televisions, a bank of video monitors, too many CDs
falling off aluminum shelves. include a half-finished vodka bottle
from brainstorming last night: giveaway posters, promo singles…
not as bad as it looks? he has a hell of a suntan.

    well hello

borrowed black and blue

he wakes up in his sister's house. Winnipeg, the month of July.
home. something like

how geometry goes somewhere and nowhere at the very same time.
rereads:
loveliness and loneliness look the same in his handwriting.

he wanted to be back where the hawks are big as his suitcase, where
the land curves up towards the sky, and now he is. mosquitoes
suspecting his body, that season. home.

*

what living does to all of us: keeps on moving, rough hand
across, catch on white sunlight. something about the heat that comes
from use, glow of pain or motion.

he wanted to explain what it *was*
not what it *was like*.

the camera panned across dust. someone was praying,
loudly. a woman was calling down curses. his lens a post-dated
evil eye.

*

twelve-hour drive and if they talked to him, it was off the record.
discussion couched in metaphor. a hawk
would simply leave when its time was over.

aren't goats kind of unsanitary
beside the hospital tent?

the nurse he was interviewing sighed,
asked a shepherd, maybe 6 years old, glints of ferocity
sharpening in dark pupils, to chase the goats out
of the frame.

...making this difference, he said.

he always felt uneasy off-air
as if caught doing something disreputable. on-camera
though

*

the air above them sliced open, if sky were a pie.
perfect plastic model went somewhere else too fast, too low.
he couldn't help but look up, every time. swoosh the sound afterwards.

they set up the shot again. *those come from outside of Vegas*, he said,
unsure why he spoke at all.

flying Winnipeg to Toronto, work beckoning.
he is too tired, gets out of bed every morning, quotes Proust
to friends who say, welcome back. he replies, *mensonge suit.*

he wears a silver-coloured jacket and trousers, pale yellow tie.
walks for a long time to the CBC building, Kensington market en route
in delighted disarray.

the walls look so solid.

*

his minder
was a captain in the secret police.
paying him.

government ministries burst, cliché, into flames. grovelling.

shakes his head. that really happened.

*

target practice: mistaken for terrorists when carrying
camera equipment.

"there had been gunfire coming from the hotel" *oh, that old excuse*

a shell
hit the 15th floor. shrapnel like coins, pennies from heaven.

concrete
flexed like a sheet of tin

the sky persistently amazed with falling.

*

on Wellington Street, a dark currency rests on his desk;
he brought it back, placed it there.

he wants a religion, something that will take all pain away—*then
how will we learn?* a clatter of windowpanes. clouds.

an open heart?

studio editing, cigarette break on the street. an ambulance goes by.

it was supposed to be
a short report. such trivial and trained seal

talk, red light, live camera. "rapid
feedback targeting."

stubs out the butt.
looks at the latest footage.

having nobody there, just the sound of wires and empty.

*

a little knot,
a series of flights in time reversal.

so this is just another discussion of loss. *haven't you had enough?*

what else is there?

personal private news

if there's too much of it, we are drowned; if there is none of it, we are
starving. is there no other word for what we lack?

the volunteers all given white rubber gloves, cheap paper masks,
a prayer of their preferred religious affiliation. bowing heads.

the empty tap coming away in his hand. how water falls upon us or
sweeps us away. how we die if it isn't surely clean.

something about compassion. put it on an aeroplane stamped
with initials, crosses or crescents.

maybe he should have kept his southern accent, stayed thoroughly
Johnny Cash, all drunk tank and motel.

there are two satisfactions: of looking without flinching, or else
the satisfaction of flinching. he can't say the latter.

he has a sudden craving for pistachios, must be something to do
with the flavour of the air this morning, its lack.

there are no new ways of describing movement in water. malarial,
with long curved beaks and words like plumage.

so does the truth comfort? or does the truth makes us despair—
he isn't sure of his job's description.

if he has to confess to a totem animal, he says "lion, or hyena"
yet knows himself a civet, nocturnal, solitary.

instead of the elephants, he finds himself watching a former model
sitting in yoga position on the roof of her jeep.

the hopeful heart: giraffe sailing through the landscape, a secretary bird,
then he's on a little airplane leaving Nairobi.

the stylist says "what bloody use are flamingos" while the driver's
guard dog lopes quietly down to the wet.

haute couture shoot on the carved veranda of the Serena Hotel; sun-lit,
palm-reflectioned, he mutters "i'm lost here."

taking a bite of the hibiscus because its petals *should* be edible, consistent
disappointment when they're not. spitting colour.

overhears "those tourists known as journalists." unable to look around;
holding to speed because the very breath depends on it.

brilliant pages for *Figaro* Magazine. he examines the prints for signs
that he's still here. he can't remember.

   the smallest spider he has ever seen, crawling across cracked leather
   of a hotel lobby desk. "the peace process crawls..."

he's there, camera flash as a coalition spokesman admits peacekeepers
tortured the rebels to death; room boiling, unsurprised.

all next day, streets empty as everyone watches football. how he wants
to join them, free his mind from everything but soaring energy.

unable to prove his equal interests in what is kept,
what is thrown away.

the river overflowing its banks: the surge, pull, he thinks "how
beautiful" but catches himself; a global language of operational synergy.

darkness

I stumble against the word unspeakable.
does everyone? the darkness
implicit.

"words cannot describe..."
but we used them, repeatedly—
what else is there? we groped our way through
the clichés
wearing sunglasses, hers very dark, knock-off Versace.

when I visited last year, we went marketing,
her hands through bags of dried red peppers saying *pilli pilli*. laughing.

slippers with the colour and look of barbecue, trailing—
ever tried these rats? tamarind pods, tied with string. for me,
she was naive explainer of wonders we hardly understood.

a single neatly-rolled white paper cone of peanuts. doorway-to-doorway,
across the packed mud. a woman held a horsehair whisk, fanned
the crumbled mud-coloured pyramid, flies to sugar.

upturned cardboard box,
men in white shirts nodding.

define
rogue and rebel, dreamer and schemer, into that past
"here".

we walked between two mountains of garlic, onion-like skin
shreds in the crowd.

the single water tap; immaculate
school uniforms worn from mud shack to concrete shed—*the school.*
pride.

of course we wanted a new system of expression,

one in which the term "unspeakable horror"
was obsolete.

a noble ambition.
don't think
that, she said to me
in a pretty café beside the Indian Ocean.
I get something, too.

sky shifting over light to dark, logic, the way we set ourselves
to resist the coming of night:

we would both prefer "unspeakable" to mean only
that about which
one cannot speak,

which must remain
a mystery,

the way the dark
shifted
as we watched the dirt road that night,
gathering itself into a shape which grew,
distinct, a secret we would look for elsewhere.

it's not about being noble, she said.
we were drinking coffee.

tiny porcelain cups, the size and shape of a saki glass.

later, there was the moon. and we

no longer there. the cups, alone.

do you see what I mean?

Kinshasa (hands on the steering wheel)

darkly she can be ok casual for days then suddenly on Thursday, eyes broken windshields behind sunglasses, driving towards Kinshasa in a '72 Mercedes listening to Lionel Ritchie. each body a separate statistic. collateral damage she adds up the numbers, makes the phone calls from what's left of. plaits her hair, swats flies. define wounded. *define this* a finger at the latest checkpoint. keeps it discreet. those polite requests for better funding, flights to Paris: ivory, coffee, ghosts. once she caught the stewardess's eye *you can see them too, huh*, didn't say anything. the unexpected she takes into her mouth, files the photos. harder to believe in, *get so tired of falling asleep*. overnight kit missing ground sheet & sleeping bag *what the fuck is that about*, she keeps going. maybe it won't end. maybe it will never end. she drives as if her mouth is filling with shards of ice so what if it is. Wonderland that's more ego than affection with a great backbeat, *how can you let go of this!* Danish colleague last week, yes hand on the ass of one of the locally fabulous. a different bar everytime, smoke-blackened greeting as Tina-Turner-wigged waitresses bring her Gold Harps, straight from the bottle between two fingers, weaves through. skin's a leash, everyone wants to be your dog. someone's real reel. misled ferocious conscience, *no idea what you'd do in similar,* no, not looking for emergency exits, she's trained to. tips back the bottle, government officers like drinking heavily... *never know who's useful.* a woman's eyelashes flash gold, are gone. kicks an expensive shin to get the dj, makes her request. shimmies with the checkerboard crowd. it's a flavour on her tongue. pieces of other lives sewn into her present tense. swallowed but not remembered faith, that warm spread through the guts etcetera. Victorian houses, commuter trains Hamilton to Toronto, how any of that continues to exist. must be what, the way you choose a shot of whiskey and close your eyes tight. took a plane away *and then what,* she nods, a reflection in the embassy glass, a Bob Marley moment. drink it all down: the rainy season, trust or some other bitter thing, *if there's a choice* Famous Grouse House all the way. the visa, signs the form. so busy avoiding too-heavy hands when she came in. small sign in font Times Roman "Please Leave Weapons With Our Receptionist While Inside Office, Pick Up at Exit" *but a camera, that, they confiscate,* one of those reporters *sans frontières,* sans everything, his exhausted laugh. *a WHO i.d. gets ya outta what* Brazzaville to Bukavu, the greens unfolding below, colours she thinks have never been seen before this moment, faith "restored to the troubled Pool region"

two 17-year-olds
yellowed eyes, purple thread,
it's a religion

machine gun Ninjas.

Cobras.
            Cocoyes.
Wild West with video game

                              precision

smoothing through families, ritual *getting down to business*. hands her an orange Kool-Aid, no way it's boiled water. ironic counterpoint? sipping dayglo, suspiciously negotiating safe passage. permission *it'll come down to cash* she'd wanted it more subtle, more lasting. if there could be some pride involved instead of dollars, suddenly imagines a grand highway opening, the 50s, women in profound dresses beside their men in hats. ribbon-cutting. puts herself in the picture and frowns. across from her, the business-suited warlord makes a tiny gesture as if waving away a fly in the coconut palms. oh Curious George had it all wrong, hummingbirds outside the suburban window. her very pregnant khaki-wearing boss sitting at the table crunching carrots. an ideal but not hers *what would make the job easier?* the serious Dutch accent, that automaton way they speak English. David Bowie coming through the opened window, tinny radio sound. *spider senses*, she thinks, *that's what*, but doesn't say. rummages through her bag, accounts, latest useless cellphone, Swiss army knife dulled in colour, package of shelled peanuts, unopened *do you mind?* says her boss and for a moment she's sure the woman means the groundnuts. the monkeynuts. what everyone's getting paid, all things considered as today's rain backs up the sink and melts the walls of Timbuktu, she hasn't even seen them yet. selfish, the only way to watch the news and not. imagine the bony animals that come from rice and human hair. she empties a bucket into a pouring driveway, nods to the neighbour's houseman. standing in the doorway watching. scorpios being water signs, in her element *rainy season's middle's different from the beginning*, someone told her. if there are snakes or what. back to television images of Mali *Is that it?* of Bob Geldof looking around. slap those mud buildings back together, no one'll notice. mud has that look to it. empties a second bucket into the driveway, the houseman's gone inside. seen enough rain though "against a white backdrop without any shadow"

one third of the women in Pool have been raped at least once.

she is typing up the word *least*. doesn't let herself pause.

what sort of truce is that?

the son of a preacher-man.

no hospitals, no schools, no churches. no homes

when everything makes her think Moscow. *that's supposed to mean?* wanting to walk down a frozen boulevard clutching Baltika #4. instead of sweating, instead of this office, she'd be bundled into fake fur, everyone else in real fox in blue, seal in pink. *so you want to be cold?* a day talking with "the assassin" age 14. *can't send me home madame, please not* because they know back home what it was he did, being told to. nickname's earned, no bravado *calls himself Samuel Oki now after the guy who was here before you.* she'll leave namesakes? children taught to murder who'll name themselves after her. absurdly Moscow. she could tell Russian friends what these children have been made into, they wouldn't flinch. they'd understand *this world exists* do what you can. she files paper, thanks him "what do they expect us to do if we give up our guns"

stolen papers must be supported by a police report.

otherwise lost or inaccessible. children under 3 years old?

waiting for the generator to come back on.

photo expression neutral, not laughing, not frowning,
not mouth open

the house unfurls itself a pawpaw, vaguely obscene fruit, pink-fleshed weed. rubbing such into her foot, early morning. sea urchin needles, black tiny dots. *nothing like pawpaw to tenderize meat,* hearing one of the wives at a barbeque. every alarm clock a kind of hinge, knees and elbows folding. the unfortunate houseguest tosses arms outward *helluva view,* every kind of cliché, she expects who, a white hunter? the fisherman door-to-door, guts snapper in the driveway. papaya antiseptic *never take your shoes off,* teva gone in a wave, could have been a rockfish. the other half, fruit for breakfast tiger-striped RnR, even her holiday's acronymed. sun lines through fingers. SPF 35 lipstick coral melting in her bag onto sunflower flip-flops wet, dark sand from the cocoa-coloured lava beach. like bitter chocolate, the kind she pays a lot of money for in Geneva when she has to be there. but now it's sunlight on the almost-black sand so almost-impossible hot on the feet. not sleeping *what d'you expect letting your guard down,* applied to her cynicism. walks down the beach, dark sand, silver water, absurdly still wanting to fall in love with "things". sky heading for aubergine. old Swedish geezer, nod to each other, passing, not holding any masks up. her dreams, *it's that I've seen too much* or closing her eyes, nothing but orange inside the eyelids intrusion of colour photographs she's neglecting. the teapot, frame with her finger, there. bitter tea, or Romans bringing vineyards to France. *no hurry in Africa madame, milk with that?* black no sugar. she was writing a letter when. she was. it's a lightening heart blue, she stops at this café because of the sign: Blue Rider. cigarettes, probably, or a barbershop, a little place with tables. loose tea in old metal pots, dinged the way her head feels, mismatched cup, saucer. Victoriana blue, fine bone china. made in. she doesn't write letters anymore, criss-crossing. *I said never mail me any,* cross with her mother not the post office *sending a bit of dash?* like Western Union. she raises her hand: greeting, or simply recognition, thinking of her own first months, how every knock on the door *ask please,* as if she were some queen of magical papers. the ice princess from a world where it snows the apartment unbeautiful but there, coddled into action. she's sleeping. increasingly elusive *the cat who walks alone* false humour for a friend who sees through, keys hidden in the ivy. such an English England even to Marks & Sparks at the Marylebone Tube. left a painting too, wrapped, her name on its tag, three-headed. she remembers sitting for a portrait *why bother with posing when we're all the same muse?* fragile determination misleading. or was it his changed direction, re-oriented metaphor *we're all dying all the time aren't we* works further under the sheets, slight foreign perfume. London traffic through horsehair, is he beside her, putting the person *she is and not was* back together "riddled with crevasses up to 30 metres wide"

the after-effects of military campaigns. observations listed:

what's called field work,

this was once at the beginning of most sentences.

swatting flies,

the polite distance of numbers

windowframe at the office *don't fly off the handle,* wood, splintered, the floor a paper performance piece. one bent metal bar, a kind of pipe. had taken her laptop home, not even usual chance. the plane left without her *just trying to scare us,* take stock *someone's succeeding, no?* selfishness or selflessness, she starts cleaning up *kpafuca,* familiar history. taking a box of papers and burning them, voices rising in the smoke, what paper can do. voices name your truth, describe *dangerous.* Iggy Pop flicks her fingers. still she'd rather choke away on. the windowframe repaired in due course not wanting to jinx it, a silent film dance routine. feathers cascading down the dress. ornithology seeming foolish, elderly holiday Brits in kneesocks. then these splendids, seven of them in the hibiscus, wise to the ways of feral cats. or a belt of tiny feathers: to become a man you club them until they fall, exhausted. *you beat the smallest parts of yourself until they're smooth*, all those games, desires, hoped-fors, worn away, simply not part anymore. replaced by something more useful. the unfantasy Lara Croft, Canada goose version, watches the blue and orange birds in the parking lot *that any of us survive*, with such delight oh-so-unlikely wires strung over their heads. trapeze artist almost falling, slum darkness, she bites her lip, cheers with the others when the boy catches himself, light swing through all their disbeliefs. close-fisted. to what point? just fly

at the end of the day, you think you're making—
she interrupts the speaker, suspended

does she say *and you, every morning waking up, you think what of your life?* gravity, or making a grab. unlit drumming, the next leap about to. she grasps the hand next to hers. wants to close her eyes but the boy, his triple somersault. what is the possible, refusing safety nets.

Notes on these poems

I wrote *A Bad Year for Journalists* while listening to Radio France
Internationale, CBC, and NPR; here's hoping public radio stays
alive. The excellent albums of Leonard Cohen, Keziah Jones, Dusty
Springfield, The White Stripes, Annie Lennox, Madonna and Johnny
Cash also provided background influence.

"press" includes passing references to Karen, an upscale residential
section of Nairobi named for writer Karen Blixen; to the Dayton boot
company of Vancouver, which started out making logging boots at the
turn of the old century and continues to produce stunningly practical
footwear; and to the mean old Blues song "Your Southern Can Is
Mine".

"what's possible" was triggered by "The Sunny Side of the World", a
review by Noah Richler in *The Globe and Mail* (April 24/04) of Pico
Iyer's latest book. See also Susan Sontag's last book, *Regarding the Pain
of Others*.

A series of reports by BBC correspondent Paul Wood inspired
"borrowed black and blue"; he describes being inside the Palestine
Hotel (where the international press lived & worked in Baghdad)
in spring 2003, when an American tank intentionally fired on the
building. Seventy-six journalists have been killed in Iraq since the war
began in March 2003. The poem includes a reference to Marcel Proust,
who was fond of sending his Parisian friends telegrams which read
"Impossible venir. Mensonge suit." A minder is assigned to accompany
foreign members of the press.

The title "i can't stand it but i'm all right" is from the song "Raja
Vocative" by The Mountain Goats. And Gold Harp is a beer brewed by
Guinness in Cameroon.

Any statistics included in these poems were correct at the time of
writing. According to Reporters Sans Frontières, 63 journalists and
media staff were killed worldwide in 2005 (not including the month of
December) compared to 53 journalists killed in 2004; on

December 7th, 2005, 68 journalists died in a single Iranian airline crash. There is also a growing fashion towards holding journalists hostage for ransom, especially in Iraq. To give a more general sense of the threat to the media: in 2003, as well as those murdered, 766 journalists were detained and at least 1,460 physically attacked or threatened. Currently, in December 2005, 115 journalists are known to be in prison because of their profession. For further information about what you can do to support freedom of the press, visit PEN at pencanada.ca and Amnesty International at amnesty.org.

Lisa Pasold has been thrown off a train in Belarus, been fed the world's best pigeon pie in Marrakech, mushed huskies in the Yukon, learned to polka at Danceland, and been cheated in the Venetian gambling halls of Ca' Vendramin Calergi. She grew up in Montreal, which gave her the necessary jaywalking skills to survive as a journalist. She currently divides her time between a tiny house in Paris and various borrowed addresses in Toronto. Her first book of poetry, *Weave*, was published by Frontenac House as part of their poetry series Quartet 2004.